I BROKE MY BRAIN

By Thomas S. Bean

The information in this book is not meant to be a substitute for medical care. If you have a medical or emotional problem, see your physician or other medical provider. You should make a medical decision only in this trusting partnership.

Edited by David Westerby and Cathy Bean

This book is dedicated to all those who have suffered from or have been influenced in any way by the dreadful and bewildering illness of clinical depression

INTRODUCTION

Depression is a serious medical condition that can be devastating to individuals and families. I can hardly imagine anything worse. I'm not talking about a bad day or week or even a rough handful of frustrating months or years when you feel you just can't catch a break. I'm talking about full-blown clinical depression.

Whether you call it major depression, major depressive disorder, a nervous breakdown, a mental breakdown, melancholy, melancholia, or just plain depression, one thing is certain. It is really, really miserable!

A lot of people (probably the majority) think this "illness" of depression is not even real and is more of a label for someone who can't cope with life. They may think it's a sorry excuse for struggling, having low self-esteem, being lazy, playing the victim role, or something of the like.

I can agree with some of this thought process since there are many people who truly do struggle, have low self-esteem, are lazy, or play the victim role, yet are not necessarily suffering from the illness of depression.

Depression involves a physiologic change among the neurotransmitters in the brain. Sometimes it is referred to as a "chemical imbalance." It affects how one feels, thinks, and behaves and can lead to a variety of emotional and physical problems. It can cause people to have trouble doing normal day-to-day activities and can make one feel as if life isn't worth living. If not properly managed it can lead to a debilitating life or may even end in suicide.

I'm not necessarily happy to say this, but I happen to know from first hand experience that there is a very distinct difference between those who are just feeling a lot of stress or are really frustrated and those that truly suffer from the illness of depression.

Unfortunately, the people who have a sincere understanding of the thoughts and feelings going on for one suffering from clinical depression are those that have had or are currently suffering from the same illness. However, this does not mean mentally healthy people cannot be helpful to those suffering from depression or other mental illness. Be grateful for your health! Do not try to live a life that can predispose you to developing depression so you can better understand it. If my neighbor wants me to help him quit smoking I do not have to become a smoker before I can help him.

The purpose of this book is to illuminate the gloomy and often confusing topic of clinical depression. Despite improving medical knowledge, new medications, and other interventions, depression rates continue to increase. It is said by many to be the most disabling medical condition.

This book is for those who have experienced or are experiencing major depression, those who love and care about sufferers of depression, and those who want to avoid becoming clinically depressed. That's a big audience.

The majority of the non-sufferers most likely have false beliefs about depression. I hope to shed some light (or should I say darkness) on the topic. Before my experience with clinical depression, I had very strong false beliefs. In my mind, depression was not an illness. I'm writing the book I wish I had read many years ago.

As I am just one of many who have suffered from depression, I do not pretend to understand everyone's situation. Likewise, I do not expect anyone reading this book to fully understand my experience. My hope is that many will avoid clinical depression because of lessons from my experiences and basic depression principles.

Why is this book any different from other books on depression? First, my personal battle with depression gives me a special perspective. Second, the book presents the most current understandings. Finally, as a physician assistant in family practice, I have helped treat hundreds of patients suffering from a variety of medical conditions, including depression.

Managing this debilitating illness can be extremely challenging. While each situation is different, the majority of the core symptoms are the same.

Patients respond differently to treatment regimens. Understanding why certain treatments work or don't work for particular people is a battle we practitioners all face. Yet, I know that this illness can be managed effectively in most, if not all, cases. I feel a personal obligation to help as many people as I can to prevent or overcome depression.

Let's get one thing straight. The opposite of depression is not happiness. The opposite of depression is the absence of the symptoms contributing to clinical depression. There are many unhappy people who do not suffer from depression.

This book will explore my first experience with clinical depression, which occurred while serving as a full-time missionary in central Florida for The Church of Jesus Christ of Latter-day Saints. I know I am not alone, as a number of other missionaries developed clinical depression, an illness not reserved to any denomination. Despite this concern, I most certainly encourage young men and women to serve missions.

For each chapter title that is IN ALL CAPITAL LETTERS, I will discuss some of the basic principles of depression. The other chapters (including the first six) will mainly include my personal life experiences.

Chapter 1: Growing up

I cannot imagine having a better childhood. I grew up with four brothers who loved to joke and play around. We supported one another as family in school, sports, and fun vacations. I remember being happy pretty much all the time. This happiness probably caused me to be ignorant of others who did not share this great joy.

I remember in grade school a classmate asking, "Why are you so high on life?" I can't remember how I answered him. I was probably a little confused and may have thought to myself, "Isn't everyone high on life?" That was my mind set. I remember being disturbed and confused when anyone would say something like "life stinks." I don't remember ever feeling like saying something like that. I just figured I was happy and everyone else was too.

If I was ever down it was usually for just a short period of time. To combat a "downer" my cure was to do something I enjoyed. This would usually help me forget I was ever down. I feel that I learned really good coping skills from a young age and was in complete control of my mood.

Sure, sometimes I fought with brothers or friends. Occasionally I got into a little mischief. Just like any other kid, I had to do things that I didn't want to do, such as chores or homework.

I was mostly very healthy, with just a handful of mild illnesses over the years. Despite these few negatives and challenges, "fun" was always just around the corner. My attitude was nearly always positive.

I had a lot of friends and could usually find something fun to do. I enjoyed trying to get better at whatever activity or sport was in season. And when it came time for work and such, I seemed to power through just fine since I knew I would probably being doing something fun shortly thereafter. Riding bikes with neighborhood friends, playing touch football or baseball, watching sports or a movie, or playing games with family or friends were regular events in my fun childhood.

My self-esteem was very high. I was confident in just about everything I did. In fact, I was quite often overconfident and considered a bragger, which some of my brothers and peers did not like. But this didn't seem to bother me much at the time.

I tried to be friends with most everyone, so I was very well liked. As a popular kid, what others thought of me may have affected me more than most. I was often praised, and this seemed to charge me to excel. I remember feeling in complete control and pushed myself to set and achieve many goals.

I was bullied only on occasion and pretty much lived by "Sticks and stones may break my bones but words will never hurt me." I would later learn that this phrase has very little truth to it.

I was quite naïve regarding "feelings." I remember as a young kid saying something really mean to my friend's sister which made her cry.

"Why are you crying," I asked, "I didn't hurt you." She then went on to explain that I "hurt her feelings." At that time I apparently didn't fully understand this.

I worked hard to get good grades in school. Learning in most school subjects did not come easily to me. I tended to have a lot of trouble focusing. It seemed like I had to work harder than most others to get good grades. I remember feeling stressed and nervous at times in school and sports, but I never remember being "depressed" for any significant amount of time.

Despite enjoying seasonal team sports the most, track and field ended up being my best sport. After dominating the short sprints in elementary school, I had aspirations of eventually breaking the world record in the 100 meter dash. As I transitioned to junior high, I realized that achieving such a lofty goal would not happen without a lot of hard work. This insight was further reinforced in high school.

I couldn't admit it until late into my senior season that the 400 meter dash would be my best event. Unfortunately, this is arguably the most painful race to run or train for.

Our team had a handful of competitive guys who pushed each other to our physical limits running interval after interval, sometimes with little rest in between. I pretty much lived by the phrases, "Pain is temporary, pride is forever" and, "If it doesn't kill you, it can only make you stronger." Both phrases seemed to inspire me, but, like the sticks and stones phrase, I would later learn are not entirely true. I put in many hours of intense workouts to maximize my strength and speed. To this day I get a little nervous whenever I watch runners in the starting blocks waiting for the gun to go off.

I wanted to go to Brigham Young University (BYU) my whole life. My parents met there, and my brothers and I cheered for the sports teams (mainly football) year after year. I knew I would have to work really hard academically to get in, as I wasn't fast enough for a track scholarship and my college entrance exam scores (ACT/SAT) were less than stellar. Reading comprehension was my low point. I attribute this to difficulty focusing due to extreme boredom trying to read things that did not interest me.

I received in the mail what I thought was a rejection letter. I had thoughts of having to go to college elsewhere. I don't know if BYU does this now, but years ago some applicants who were not accepted to start college in the fall semester had the option to start early in the summer term. If things went well, the student could continue school in the fall semester. I was given this option and so just one week after graduating from high school in June I had to dive into college. I was excited to go but would have preferred a summer break before the fall semester.

For whatever reason, I was selected to live on an "honors floor." My roommate was a chemistry genius, and I felt like I was surrounded by many other intellectual stallions. Everyone was talking about all of the "AP credits" that they received from honors classes in high school. I had zero AP credits. I don't remember ever being in an "honors class" in high school, although I tended to be in the more advanced math classes. I also don't remember talking to many others who had to attend summer term, although I'm sure there were plenty who wanted to keep it on the down low.

To add to the intimidation, I didn't sign up for any of the "typical" freshman classes such as biology, religion, history, or other general education that would make it convenient to study with other freshmen around me. I made the mistake of allowing my father to sign me up for classes such as anatomy and child development. I did have a half-credit tennis class that was enjoyable and obviously much simpler. I most certainly aced that one, pun intended.

I remember the first class of child development when the instructor asked how many freshmen were taking the class and my hand and two or three others went up. He then stated that this is a very hard class and that we will have to study really hard to get a decent grade. That wasn't the most comforting introduction.

In anatomy, I had to learn so many things so quickly that I wasn't sure I could keep up there either. I already felt burned out graduating from high school just a week before. Being a clueless new freshman, I was too intimidated to figure out how to change any of my classes. I don't know how I actually found the time to have fun during that condensed summer term, but I have good memories outside of studying.

The last couple of weeks with finals approaching, my stress level accelerated. I studied hour upon hour, which was far more than I had ever had done before. I felt like I was going crazy and that I really wanted to pause the world for a long time and take a break. I had fleeting thoughts of really wanting a punching bag. After all the hard work and probably some luck I pulled through the tough classes and got that much needed break before the fall semester.

When fall semester arrived, I roomed with my best friend from high school. Unlike summer term, I was in a program where several of my dorm-mates had a lot of the same general education classes. I was still intimidated by most other students as I continued to feel inferior scholastically. Pathetically, I still had a fear of changing classes. Some of my afternoon classes cut into track and field. My chances of making the team as a walk on would have improved had I just made some simple class changes.

We had good camaraderie within our dorm and had plenty of fun to go along with all the studies. I eventually was successful in track, although I had a lot more fun competing in all the intramural activities like flag football and basketball. Similar to high school, I was fond of a few young women and did some dating, but nothing serious.

I was fortunate that I didn't run into many serious trials. There was a time when I was injured with a pulled hamstring, and I really had some trouble in classes during the winter semester, but any low mood was very temporary.

I really felt like I grew a lot physically, mentally, emotionally, and spiritually throughout my first year of college. I had periods of stress all along the way as I set and achieved goals. There were ups and downs, but I can't think of any extended period of time that I felt depressed. As far as I was concerned and had been taught, stress was a good thing. We're here to challenge ourselves and improve. We have to go out of our comfort zone to get better and excel at things. I felt like life was moving along just fine.

Chapter 2: Called to Serve

Ever since I was a little kid, I planned on serving a full-time mission for my church when I reached the age of 19. I remember telling people that I wanted to go to Japan. I'm not really sure why. Maybe from watching "Big Bird Goes To Japan." Or maybe because my 7th-grade English class wrote to pen pals (from a school class) in Japan for a few months. This desire must have faded since I did not study Japanese in high school (took Spanish). You see, I had been told that the Spanish class was easier than the other languages. With less pressure studying a foreign language I could put more time into sports and other fun activities.

During the winter semester at BYU, I was excited as many of my friends and acquaintances were receiving calls to serve as full-time missionaries. Finally, my call came. I was pretty sure I would serve in a foreign land. I gathered my friends into my dorm room and had my parents on the phone as I opened my call to serve in the Florida, Tampa Mission, speaking English.

I had written in my journal a couple of months before receiving my call that I was excited to serve the Lord. I mentioned not having to worry about school, homework, studying for tests, track, or girls. This anticipation may have hurt me during the last couple months of the winter semester. I had difficulty focusing on my studies and other activities.

I was surprised while looking back in my journal that I actually did mention feeling somewhat depressed during this tough time. I think it is human nature to remember the good times and to forget the rough times.

I don't think I was very discouraged about not serving a foreign mission. I would have to say that I was more surprised than discouraged. I was somewhat relieved also that I wouldn't need to learn another language. I would soon learn that Florida is plenty foreign to me, with foreign people and languages aplenty.

I remember being rather excited and nervous at the same time before leaving to serve the Lord for two years. Smartly, I took it easy with quality rest and relaxation for several weeks before leaving home again.

The Missionary Training Center (MTC) in Provo, Utah provided a terrific experience. As an English-speaking missionary,

11

I was to be in the MTC for just 3 weeks before going to Florida. Early on, I was called to serve as the district leader of about 12 missionaries. I felt a little added pressure with this early calling, but not too much. It would last only a few weeks anyway.

My companion was from a little town in Arizona, and we got along great. My mission president and his wife were called to the mission on an emergency basis since the previous mission president had passed away unexpectedly. They had already been in the mission field for a few months and then came back to the MTC to learn what they were supposed to have been doing the last few months. It was a unique experience to meet my Mission President and his wife in the MTC before going into the mission field.

My excitement grew stronger after meeting them and their comments to me and the others made us even more eager to serve in Florida. He stressed that he wanted the mission to be the highest baptizing mission in the southeast region. I don't remember if he used the quote "It ain't braggin' if ya done it" in the MTC or shortly after being in the field, but I knew he meant business (the Lord's business). He was an intense individual. He had a military background and the mission rules were to be followed to the letter of the law. So after three weeks in the MTC, it was time to go to central Florida to help spread the gospel.

Chapter 3: Into the Mission Field

I was excited to see my mission president and his wife when they greeted me and the other missionaries at the airport in Florida. We had a full load, heading to the mission home in Tampa. I happened to sit in the front seat, between my mission president, who was driving, and his wife, on the passenger side. I looked out the window and saw the stadium where the Tampa Bay Buccaneers play. I was mostly kidding when I asked the president, "So, do we get to go to any Buccaneers games?" He slowly turned his head toward me with a disturbing confused look and then he put his eyes back on the road and said, "No, Elder Bean, we don't do that." Many of us laughed at this later, but we knew without question that the president had high expectations for us to work very hard and that there was no time to mess around.

As far as I was concerned, mission presidents across the world were about the same. I would later hear that the next mission president was more of a huggable, grandfather-like figure.

From the get go, I was a very happy, high energy, fireball greenie (new missionary). My first companion, my trainer, was an extremely hard worker from Idaho with a farming background. With my nature of pushing myself to achieve challenging goals, I felt pleasantly pushed by my trainer. Like most missionaries coming from the MTC, I probably felt that I knew what I was doing more so than I actually did. I was quickly humbled in every way.

As an athlete, I didn't think I would have any trouble keeping up with my companion on a bike. With nearly 100-degree temperatures and 100% humidity in Tampa, biking was not the most pleasurable experience, but I adapted over time. My companion encouraged me to go above and beyond the call of duty. We had a program to memorize the six discussions and many scriptures. Awards were given after passing off these discussions and scriptures to missionary leaders. As an "overachiever," I wanted to pass everything off as quickly as possible.

My trainer encouraged me to get up an hour early (5:30 instead of 6:30) to work on the memorization. He had been getting up early also. Through this hard work I passed everything off much quicker than most missionaries, and I prided myself in this.

Over the first few months in the mission field, I things were going great, and I was coping well. After all the hard work on a daily basis, I always looked forward to Monday, which was our preparation day (P-Day). On this day we had some personal time away from our intense missionary work schedule. I usually tried to get other missionaries to play basketball or do another physical activity. I also enjoyed reading and writing letters to/from friends and family. Lastly, it was the day for laundry and shopping for groceries. Fortunately, with our limited wardrobe and having generous church members to feed us, neither of these activities were complicated or stressful.

My overall health seemed to be just fine except for my "nervous stomach." I remember a time in elementary school spending the night at a Filipino friend's house where I wouldn't eat his mom's cooking. I felt really bad that I offended her and other family members. From this experience and possibly others, I must have developed a fear of not being able to eat at other people's houses. In the mission field we had a dinner appointment nearly every night with one of the church members. At least I was in the United States, so I didn't come across a lot of unfamiliar foods.

In my first area, my companion and I taught many discussions, and I felt like I was thoroughly learning the gospel as I was teaching. We had high hopes for a lot of our investigators since they all seemed really excited about the gospel during our discussions.

Almost all of our investigators were found by going door to door or from media referrals (people who ordered a video, a Bible, or Book of Mormon from a TV commercial). Because of this, very few of them had a connection with local church members. Most of them had difficulty making and keeping commitments, and many would come across "anti-Mormon" literature from family or friends.

This was extremely discouraging to me and my companion as the people we were teaching tended to "fizzle out" despite our strong efforts to share the gospel. I think I took this harder than I should have. I even questioned the strength of my faith, when in all reality, the investigators were not prepared at that time to embrace the gospel fully.

I would compare most of the people we taught to a category of people mentioned in "The Parable of the Sower" from the Bible. Some of these people got excited about the gospel initially, but did not have a strong foundation. They were on "rocky soil" and struggled to make and keep commitments. Up to this point, I experienced the expected ups and downs that my father predicted I would have. Depression had no place in me yet.

The first mention of the word "depressing" in my mission journal had nothing to do with my mood. It was in reference to the poor, humbling, potentially dangerous parts of town. I had voiced frustration in my journal, but never mentioned feeling depressed. At about that time, my companion and I made a cute little video that I sent home. My mom commented on how happy and healthy I looked.

I remember a missionary in our district who had an appointment with a doctor. I was confused because I didn't think he was sick. I asked him about his medical concern and he said it was "a mental thing." I didn't know what that meant. Looking back, I think he was visiting a therapist, possibly on a regular basis. I didn't feel comfortable delving into his "mental thing" and I don't think he was comfortable talking about it either. This may have been the first time I had interacted with someone who I knew was seeing a mental health specialist.

My understanding of people who saw mental health specialist was that they are messed up and crazy. I was probably the most ignorant and naïve 19-year-old regarding mental illness. My childhood had very little significant turbulence. I do not recall any of my family members going through any kind of depression or other significant psychological issues. I'm sure it was around me at various times growing up, but I was oblivious to it.

I remember even being confused the first time I watched the movie "Top Gun." At the start of the movie, Tom Cruise (Maverick) and Anthony Edwards (Goose) were in the same plane. Another pilot (Cougar) was also in the air when enemy fighter planes appeared to be attacking. One of the enemies had an opportunity to shoot down Cougar's plane. During this time Cougar was having some kind of a "panic attack," and although he wasn't fired at, his emotional instability made him unable to function as a pilot. Maverick had to basically "take him by the hand" to make sure he landed safely.

Because of this experience Cougar turned in his wings. I had no idea what a "panic" or "anxiety attack" was. I was clueless about any mental or emotional illness. Don't get me wrong. I had experienced stress and nervousness at times in my life, but I did not understand it could happen so dramatically as to essentially shut down one's ability to function.

Very early on in my first mission area, I had the crazy idea of flying off a high jump on my bike. Not only did I have the idea, but I actually went for it. This was at least the second time I tried to physically break my brain. The first was just before the age of two when I was cheering for my dad at a softball game and fell off the top bleachers (14 feet high) and landed on my head. My right arm was sandwiched between my head and the ground and at least somewhat cushioned the blow. I broke both the ulna and the radius (forearm bones) and spent some time in a cast.

Now, about 18 years later as a missionary, I broke my right collar bone. My body literally bounced off the pavement. My bike helmet (which broke from the accident) saved my life or at least some serious neurological damage. I had to be transferred to another area that had a car for a little while and then shortly got back to my first area. Fortunately we were able to get a car there temporarily. My first companion was then transferred and called to be a zone leader somewhere in Orlando.

My next companion was a big, tough guy from Canada and we were back on bikes as I had healed up well enough. We didn't get along quite as well, but we continued to have some success over the next month before I was to be transferred to Bradenton. My companion had quite the reaction when he found out where I was going. He said one of the missionaries in that area "was crazy" and took medication for it. We were both hopeful that "the crazy missionary" would be transferred away and that I would serve with the other missionary.

Fortunately, I did get to serve with "the other missionary." It was apparent that he didn't get along with "the crazy missionary" since shortly after I got to the area he rode his bike with his hands in the air and yelled, "I'm freeeeeeeeee."

Chapter 4: My First Transfer

The mission experience continued to go well in my second area. I got along with my companion well, and we had good success. There were the expected ups and downs, but I continued to learn and grow as we shared the gospel.

I remember teaching a man with schizophrenia, an eye-opening experience for me. He was very nice, but it was kind of odd that he thought he was broadcasting our discussions to large audiences somewhere. This may have been my first significant contact with someone who I knew for sure was mentally ill. I mentioned in my journal that I was learning how to take pressure really well.

I had an unexpected experience during the next zone conference. My mission president told me about a friend of mine who was driving with his mother to the MTC to serve a mission in the Dominican Republic, when an auto crash occurred, and both died. I had a delayed reaction after hearing the news, and I eventually broke down and cried. One of the assistants to the president did a really good job comforting me and I seemed to recover from this rather quickly.

Although probably unrelated, a few days after this, I woke up feeling really sick. On the same day, I received a phone call from the mission president. I was to be transferred to Kissimmee (by Orlando) and was also called to be a district leader. I really didn't see that coming. A typical district in our mission at that time consisted of about 4-6 missionaries. A zone usually consisted of about 3 or 4 districts or about 12-16 missionaries.

I remember being quite overwhelmed, as I had been a junior companion for my first several months and now was to be a senior companion and a district leader in an unfamiliar area. Being physically sick at that time didn't help. My companion gave me a blessing and I got ready to go to my next area. This was the only transfer in my entire mission that I couldn't find a local church member to take me. So there I was, feeling really sick and riding the Greyhound bus to Kissimmee. On top of all this, it happened to be Thanksgiving.

Chapter 5: Leadership

After moving to my new area, my illness didn't leave, and I developed a nasty cough. I was able to see a doctor, had a chest x-ray, and was diagnosed with bronchitis. I was given a medication and cough syrup. I mentioned in my journal that I was a bit depressed. I don't know if it was one of the medications that caused it, but I felt really strange, like I was often in a dream state. The doctor thought it might be the cough syrup, but I'm not so sure.

Over the next few days, I got feeling well again. Upon recovering, I dove back into the work at full force. I was back to waking up early to have more time to memorize scriptures. This new area was talked up highly, as it was one of the most successful areas in the mission over the past year or so. I think this put a little more pressure on me to make sure the success in this area remained high.

Unfortunately, we were not having much success during my time. I felt like I was falling behind. I was uncharacteristically hard on the other missionaries during a district meeting. I don't think it really affected any of us much, as we all got along great at a dinner appointment shortly after. I remember us all having a laughing attack at one point.

I mentioned in my journal that missionary work is exciting and that I love it. As the days went on, I seemed to continue to be hard on myself and probably put too much energy into memorizing the scriptures to receive all the awards. I had been working so hard but was disappointed in not finding as much success as I hoped.

My feelings fluctuated greatly. I felt frustration, and I felt my faith was too weak. We just weren't having any success. The ward I was in was letting me down and my companion did not seem to want to work. On the other hand, I felt personal growth on a daily basis. That kept me motivated. I even thought how tough it would be to end my mission. I was all over the place.

I felt a little upswing when I heard I would be training a new missionary as my next companion in the same area.

Chapter 6: Training a Newby

I almost fell over when the new missionary showed up. It turned out to be a kid from my hometown. We were even in some of the same seminary classes. On top of being able to talk about hometown stuff, this greenie seemed to have some of the same fire that I came into the mission with.

We had good immediate success together in finding people to teach. I was continuing to feel growth spiritually on a daily basis. What happened next was unpredictable.

One day I woke up feeling sick and fatigued. A few days later I felt depressed and troubled. Every emotion was flowing through my body, and I applied Nephi's "O wretched man that I am" to the way I was feeling.

I'm not sure why I was being so hard on myself. Maybe it was because our last baptism was so long ago. Probably my personal expectations were far too high. Objectively, I was doing fine work. Several other missionaries had complimented me for my great attitude, knowledge, confidence, and overall missionary skills. I was told by others that I would be a great leader in the mission field. Lack of baptisms gnawed at me.

I felt guilty and I seemed to question my own worthiness to be a missionary. I even expressed this concern to my mission president and got a weird vibe from him over the next few months.

To add to my strange feelings, on one occasion a married couple—each a returned missionary—told stories from their missions and some "Mormon folk lore" that sounded pretty far out. Another person added stories that were even more far fetched. This event may have spiritually "weirded me out."

In one of the stories, a missionary died and later came from the spirit world to give another missionary a special blessing to essentially finish his mission through him. After this visit, I had some bizarre thoughts about my friend who passed away before his mission possibly doing something similar. Looking back, it's hard for me to believe that I would have put serious thought into the things I heard that night. But with my mood having unpredictable swings, I shouldn't be surprised that I was being affected by things that shouldn't really matter.

CHAPTER 7: WHAT IS THE CAUSE OF DEPRESSION?

If I were to conduct a survey asking people what the most likely cause of depression is, I think the most common answer would be stress. Some of the most stressful experiences may include divorce, losing a job, chronic illness, financial problems, unexpected loss of a family member or friend, moving, failing to achieve certain goals, physical abuse, or emotional trauma. It would be difficult to argue that these stressors do not at least contribute to depression. But does something like this have to happen to bring on depression? Can one get depressed without anything major happening at all?

Is stress always a bad thing? I agree with the findings that some stress is good (eustress). Society focuses on stress being negative or bad (distress). Is the negative stress always bad? Don't we grow from our challenging experiences that include negative stress?

"If it doesn't kill you, it can only make you stronger." I wish that this had more truth to it. I can see it inspiring people at times, but I wouldn't quote it to anyone with multiple sclerosis, Lou Gehrig's disease, terminal cancer, or the like. Similarly, I wouldn't use with anyone suffering from clinical depression.

Does selfishness play a role in depression? A friend of mine at church mentioned that depression is selfish because you only think about yourself. I can see this being a possibility but I'm sure there are plenty of people suffering from depression who are not selfish. Does one think more about him- or herself after having clinical depression? I don't recall thinking much about other people during the times I was sick with a nasty cold or the flu. Should we expect a big difference from one suffering from depression?

Will selfishness always lead to depression? I can think of many selfish people who are not depressed. They're mostly arrogant jerks, but rarely clinically depressed. In other words, I don't think selfishness can take credit for being the main cause of depression.

Lots of medical conditions run in families. Depression is certainly one of them. Do family members act and think similarly and so the pattern of their lives makes them more likely to get depressed? Do certain people have a lower threshold for this condition? I would agree to both of these possibilities.

Women are more likely to be diagnosed with depression. Are more women depressed or are they just more likely to seek treatment? Could it be related to their hormone fluctuation?

Some risk factors that could increase the chance of depression would include having depressive symptoms at a younger age. A history (or family history) of anxiety disorder, a personality disorder, or post-traumatic stress disorder also increase the chance of becoming depressed. Drug or alcohol abuse may reflect self treatment for depression, but could also cause or worsen depression. I imagine just about any kind of addiction could lead to depression.

Some medications, including those to treat blood pressure, may have a side effect of depression. Certain personality traits such as having low self-esteem or being overly dependent, self-critical, pessimistic, or a perfectionist can lead to or contribute to depression.

The susceptibility to develop depression varies greatly. To explain this, let's take a simpler illness such as the common cold. Patient A is bothered by a sore throat, a runny and stuffy nose, and a cough. These symptoms go away after one to two weeks, and patient A is back to normal. Let's say patient B has the same exposure and picks up the same virus that patient A picked up. Patient B happens to be really prone to getting a sinus infection. Instead of patient B's symptoms going away in one to two weeks, he or she develops a secondary bacterial infection (sinusitis) that won't go away for several weeks and may require antibiotics to help clear it up. Let's say patient C has the same exposure but happens to suffer from asthma. This patient gets short of breath, wheezes, has a worse cough, and just like patient B doesn't get better for a long time. Even worse, patient C then develops bronchitis or pneumonia. I haven't even talked about individualized immune function but I think you get the point.

Each patient has the same exposure and is infected with the same virus, but each has a different health outcome. Similarly, two people can have the same sun exposure but one may have a more significant sunburn. One may develop skin cancer in the future, and the other may not.

Why is one athlete more prone to injury than another athlete in the same sport? How about soldiers who are exposed to the same traumas and tragedies? Are they all affected exactly the same? Will each soldier later be diagnosed with PTSD (post traumatic stress disorder) or just some of them?

So, are some people more prone to depression than others? I would have to say yes.

Can hormones play a role in depression—not only a certain time of the month for some women but certain periods of life such as menopause? You wouldn't need to talk to many women to get a more solid answer to this question.

Are people who have had a heart attack more likely to get depressed? Absolutely. There's plenty of research to support this. What about other medical conditions such as HIV, cancer, or chronic pain? Yes. Could any combination of these issues contribute to or worsen depression? There is no doubt. Does that mean anyone who has any or all of these conditions automatically gets depressed? No.

What about the weather? Some people suffer from something called SAD (seasonal affective disorder). This occurs due to lack of light. Are some people even the opposite and get depressed during the hot summer when there's plenty of light? Yes, but obviously from a different physiologic mechanism. What about someone who has lost a close relative at a certain time of the year? Could this person tend to get more depressed around this time of year because of the loss? Absolutely.

What about a combination of genetics, a sunless winter, a hormone issue, the feelings of failure from an unmet expectation, and a traumatic life event? Who wants to sort that one out? Simply, the "cause" of depression is not always known. This would be a good reason not to pass judgments on others because you don't know what's really going on inside the brain of the depressed individual.

It's chicken or egg time. Does someone become depressed because one or more of the triggers happens, and then a chemical imbalance of the brain follows? Or does someone's brain have a chemical imbalance first, and this causes the individual to get depressed? Does one have a pattern of negative thoughts causing brain changes or does a change of the brain pattern cause the negative thoughts? Is it always the same? I doubt it.

Consider cognitive distortions. A few examples are polarized thinking, jumping to conclusions, discounting the positive, personalization, filtering, and overgeneralization. Could one or more of these negative, distorted thought patterns lead to clinical depression? Of course. In the book "Feeling Good" by David D. Burns, cognitive distortions are portrayed as a main cause of mood disorders. Could one of more of these distorted thinking patterns occur due to a major, stressful event or other negative experience in life? I would have to say yes.

How does someone get locked into this type of thinking? Why would anyone choose to think negatively most or all of the time? Is something good supposed to come out of it? Not really. If you bang your head against the wall repeatedly and complain of getting headaches, you should stop banging your head against the wall. Logically, it sounds so simple.

How about perfectionism or OCD (obsessive compulsive disorder)? Could either of these lead to depression? Or does someone who is depressed develop this type of thinking? Anyone who expects personal perfection or perfect cleanliness is most assuredly being set up for failure. Expecting perfection in others will most assuredly lead to disappointment and/or depression as well. A similar lose-lose situation is the person who has to keep washing his or her hands (OCD) over and over because they can never get clean enough.

How about repeated head trauma (concussions) leading to depression? I'm sure this could play a role but it certainly doesn't explain all of the people who have had multiple concussions and are not depressed. The NFL is currently under scrutiny because of concussions and the connection to a variety of neurological and psychological problems (including depression and suicide) that may be stemming from them. This may be a piece to the puzzle, but will not explain the many people who have never had a concussion that come down with clinical depression.

How about just working too hard for too long without a break? This is sometimes called burnout. We all know what can happen to a car during a race if it doesn't take a pit stop. Can overdoing it in life cause depression? Can a runner or other athlete overdo it and train too hard? Sure. This could lead to injury or burnout. Burnout is most commonly a mental thing, even for repetitive physical tasks. So, can someone overdo mental tasks just as much as physical ones? Of course.

So it would make sense that someone who tries to do too much mentally, physically, emotionally, or even spiritually could "crack," "snap," "break," or whatever you want to call it.

I, who didn't think these types of things could happen to me, must have ignored all warning signs, thinking that pushing myself with the "more is better" mindset would ultimately help me to improve, similar to working really hard physically to improve in running.

This chapter may be filled with too many questions and not enough answers. I hope it at least helps to open your mind to understanding that there are many possible triggers that could cause mental harm (such as depression). Just like there are numerous ways to be injured physically, we need to realize that not all mental illness comes about from the same cause.

Chapter 8: My First Car Area

On my next transfer I was excited to get a new start. It was nice to finally be in a car area also. Over the course of the mission I spent 17 months in a bike area and only 7 months in a car area despite about half of the areas having a car. It was also a unique situation as I was the area leader (senior companion?) and district leader but my companion was the zone leader. This caused quite the clash between us. My companion didn't seem to smile much or ever seem to be in a good mood much of the time. This certainly may have put a damper on my mood.

The church members in the area seemed very supportive. With that level of support, normally I would be excited to go forth and work hard (which we did), but I just wasn't feeling right. I felt I needed to get my "greenie fire" attitude back. I mentioned in my journal that I'm "Still feeling weird and going crazy. I need to talk to the mission president." I continued to feel "weird" the next few days and mentioned in my journal that "Something big will happen soon." I may have had a decent day or so but took a nap one day which is not at all normal for me. The day after this I felt as badly as ever. My journal entries were getting more disturbing by the day. 3/19/96: "Coo, coo, going crazy. At or near bottom of roller coaster. Pathetic district meeting. I have a cruddy attitude and it needs to be deleted from my mind."

I mentioned in a district meeting that I loved my companion which was more of a hope than anything since we really weren't getting along. My mood continued to flounder between fair and poor on a day-to-day basis. I was hopeful for a positive change on the next transfer day. Unfortunately, I got word that I was to remain with my companion for another month.

I remember having small spurts of optimism but mostly felt frustrated and depressed. If there weren't enough red flags popping up, the following journal entry should have made it pretty obvious that I was sick. 3/29/96: "Going nuts. Something needs to happen. Feeling fruitless. I'm feeling like I'm going to disappear. I can't comprehend a lower low than I am on." In the following entry I stated that the low hit the bottom. I must have spoken with the mission president or his wife or both as it was planned for me to go to see "some counselor guy" from a nearby area to help me get feeling well again.

Throughout my life until this point I would say I was a very positive person. Any journal entry before my mission and the first several months of my mission were filled with positive notions. Now that I was feeling so bad all the time, I didn't really have anything positive to say. Over time, I think it is human nature to forget about most of the negatives and remember most of the positives. If this were not the case, I don't believe a typical mother would ever decide to give birth to another child.

CHAPTER 9: WHY IS DEPRESSION SO PREVALENT?

Depression has been called the common cold of mental illness (probably due to its prevalence). I think this comparison is terrible because a common cold is very predictable. You know what symptoms will occur and you know about when you will recover. With depression, you know you will feel awful, but you rarely know how severe it will be or how long it will last. When you're sick with a cold you physically look sick and people understand that you need to lie down and rest because they've been sick like that before and know what needs to be done to get better as quickly as possible. With depression you may look normal (not sick), and so it's very difficult to explain to your friends why you don't want to do anything.

Why are the rates of depression so prevalent and continuing to increase? I remember being at a pharmaceutical dinner and having a discussion with a psychiatrist about this question. His theory is that our brains may not be made to process all of the demands of this day and age. Things didn't used to be so complicated. If you go back in time far enough, well before the alarm clock, a man's duty was pretty much to kill a large animal every now and again so his family could be fed. The woman's duty was to prepare food and probably not a whole lot more than that. We fell asleep when we were tired and woke up when we were rested.

Over time, our way of life has become much more stressful and competitive. Alarm clocks, deadlines, having to be in certain places at certain times, constant communication with so many people (including social media), computers, other electronic devices, work issues, school issues, financial difficulties, and relationships are just some of these stressors. Are our brains more vulnerable than years ago? Hopefully the medical community will be better able to determine the cause(s) of depression in the future.

Chapter 10: Things Getting Darker

So I am spending another month with a companion that I've struggled to get along with. Looking back at this, there is no question that I was in the midst of a clinical depression. At the time, I was in complete denial. I was probably thinking that I was having a unique mission experience. I've never experienced significant depression before, and I've never served a mission before. Surely these feelings will go away as I continue to serve. Right? This isn't abnormal at all. Right? Many before have suffered from depression and I should be able to snap out of it on my own. Right? All I have to do is change my attitude. Right? I should just think happy thoughts and I'll be fine. Right?

I visited a family doctor—a local church member to discuss my depression symptoms. I put on the "I'm-feeling-just-fine face" and refused to admit I was depressed. He mentioned that to be diagnosed with depression, you have to be suffering from the symptoms for two weeks straight. I rationalized in my head that I had some okay days along the way and couldn't have possibly been depressed for two straight weeks. Looking back, I had been depressed for several weeks but couldn't admit it to myself.

I seemed to get a little "upper" after an interview with the mission president and his wife. They talked about the need for compromise between my companion and me. I convinced myself that my problems were stemming from my companionship and that things would get better as we resolved our differences.

At one point, I remember overhearing a couple of missionaries discussing how they were either taking, or had taken, the medication "Prozac." One of them mentioned how it made him feel so much better. I remember specifically not wanting to talk to either of them about this because I just assumed they were "crazy."

My overall memory of the area is most certainly dark. My emotions were tending to fluctuate more than usual, most certainly more on the downside with just a few pockets of feeling okay and having good experiences.

I had a discussion with another elder in the district, and he expressed some of his previous psychological challenges. I mentioned in my journal, "That elder needs help." Looking back, there's no question that I was far more in need of help at the time than this other elder.

Despite all the low points, I apparently had enough small breakthroughs of feeling okay to at least keep a little bit of optimism and hope for feeling well again. I mentioned in my journal that although I would have just a small "up" in mood for a short time, I was still recovering. This journal entry is somewhat contradictory to my depression denial since using the term recovery suggests some kind of injury or illness. In other words, I must have come to grips that I was battling depression. Still I did not feel comfortable seeking any outside help. More than likely, I convinced myself that as long as I was following all mission rules and doing my best I would surely snap out of this awful funk.

I was fortunate to have a period where I felt significantly better than expected for a few days. I felt the "old greenie fire" coming back. I was feeling the gift of knowledge during this time as we found a mother with twin boys who were very receptive to the gospel. Looking back, this period of good days may have even been something called a "hypomania" which would be equivalent to a milder form of a "mania" that occurs in "bipolar disorder" (also called manic depressive disorder or bipolar depression). On the flip side of this happy period, I remember having a crying spell for which I do not recall a particular trigger. I would consider this crying spell bizarre and disturbing, and I tried to put it out of my mind. It is not recorded in my mission journal.

My mood dropped back down rather quickly, and I had a very frustrating experience with a leader. Several companionships had been tracting (going door to door) and were to meet back at a particular time. My companion and I happened to get back first and waited for the other companionships. Naturally, I was tired and so I took my shoes off, lied on the couch, and kicked my feet up for a few minutes. When the other companionships met up with us one of the leaders gave me a scolding look and later pulled me aside to tell me how upset he was with me for relaxing. He said my relaxing was a bad example to other missionaries, especially those who did not have a strong work ethic. Looking back, I can understand his concern, but it still bothered me.

Are we all supposed to be workaholics and never take any time to rest, even for a few minutes when feeling weary? I honestly do not know how much of a role this experience played in my mood dropping back down, but a couple days later I had an entire day of feeling "weird" and "sick." It was not the kind of

sick that has an obvious cause such as an upper respiratory
infection or a flu bug. I couldn't put a finger on it at the time, but
my depression was getting worse.

CHAPTER 11: HOW IS DEPRESSION DIAGNOSED?

Diagnosing depression can be quite a challenge since each patient's situation may vary significantly. One's depression can be mild, moderate, severe, or maybe not at all (misdiagnosis). For some patients, the chief complaint is depression; others don't know why they feel terrible. The diagnosis is not cut and dried, like having hepatitis or HIV (you've got it or you don't). You can't leave a urine sample and find out a minute later if it's positive or negative for depression. It's not like hypertension, diabetes, underactive thyroid, or elevated cholesterol, where the diagnosis can be made with a number value from a lab test or a blood pressure cuff.

Interestingly, there actually are some newer blood tests that may suggest which (if any) antidepressant(s) may be most effective for a patient, but these expensive blood tests are not part of today's main-stream medicine. Nor would I consider it main-stream medicine to order a really expensive brain scan (such as a PET scan or MRI) on anyone who feels depressed to see if a pattern is found to suggest clinical depression.

Depression is essentially diagnosed by an interview, possibly some questionnaires, and sometimes a gut impression. One of the biggest clues that a patient might be depressed is when the patient says, "I think I'm depressed." Even so, such an admission is not definitive; other factors should be considered.

A questionnaire sounds pretty helpful, and often is. But if a patient is in denial, he or she may not answer the questionnaire in a manner that suggests depression. On the flip side, a questionnaire may suggest depression in a situation where a patient that tends to exaggerate may not actually be sick.

In most cases, a questionnaire is very helpful. Of the many screening questionnaires for depression, the PHQ-9 (Patient Health Questionnaire) is one of the best, since it is short and simple.

The way these nine questions are answered usually is a good indication of who is suffering from clinical depression. This self assessment takes into account how one has felt over the past two weeks.

To answer each question, you give a number value from zero to three. Zero would mean not at all; 1 would mean several

31

days; 2 would mean more than half the days; and 3 would mean every day (or nearly so).

These are the following statements of the questionnaire:
•**1**. Having little interest or pleasure in doing things (anhedonia).
•**2**. Feeling down, depressed, or hopeless.
•**3**. Having trouble falling or staying asleep or sleeping too much.
•**4**. Feeling tired or having little energy.
•**5**. Poor appetite or over eating.
•**6**. Feeling bad about yourself or that you are a failure or have let yourself or your family down.
•**7**. Having trouble concentrating on things, such as reading the newspaper or watching television.
•**8**. Moving or speaking so slowly that other people would notice, or being so fidgety or restless that you have been moving around a lot more than usual.
•**9**. Having thoughts of hurting yourself or that you would be better off dead.

When I started feeling depressed as a missionary, it was only natural for me to think that I must have done something bad (guilty feelings). Abe Lincoln once said, "When I do good, I feel good. When I do bad, I feel bad. That's my religion." While feeling so badly as a missionary, I couldn't help but think of previous mistakes that I had made in life. I felt bad about them even though I knew I could do nothing about the past. It really messed with my head.

Other symptoms that are common with depression include isolation, anger, anxiety, constant worry, fear of change, becoming more passive, tentative, or avoidant, feeling out of control, feeling damned or cursed, having feelings of "why me?" or "it's not fair", having trouble relaxing, and having a tendency to let things slide.

Depression is typically worst in morning. At times, this may be partially due to sleep quality. In most cases, a depressed patient will have decreased restorative sleep and increased dreaming. Sometimes diagnosing a depressed patient is very challenging. It is not uncommon for a patient to be complaining of physical problems such as back pain or headaches, when in all

32

reality these physical symptoms are stemming from clinical depression.

To meet the diagnostic criteria for depression, it must be severe enough to cause noticeable problems in day-to-day activities, such as work, school, social activities, or relationships with others. Symptoms can be based on your own feelings or may be based on the observations of someone else. One clue much more common among youth is self-mutilation such as cutting.

Feeling depressed, having a bad day, or feeling down for a little while is not the same as having clinical depression. In fact, temporarily feeling depressed can be a healthy emotional response that something isn't right. To make an analogy, pain is most certainly not pleasant but can be very helpful. For instance, if you put your hand on a hot stove, your hand would probably get severely burned if you didn't have pain to tell you to remove it.

Although depression is not the same as pain, depression symptoms need to persist to have clinical significance. A patient needs to be significantly depressed for at least two weeks straight to be considered clinically depressed.

Chapter 12: Another New Start

I received a transfer to an area near Orlando. I had mentally chalked up my times of depression to being with a companion I didn't get along with, and was looking forward to starting fresh with another companion. It turned out that I was familiar with my new companion as I had met him at a previous meeting. I was excited to serve with him. He was a happy, fun-loving Tongan. We lived with another companionship that got along great together. The area was also very close to my third area (Kissimmee). I had hopes that some of the people I had taught a few months previous might decide to be baptized and that I might even have permission to attend.

Initially, I was feeling optimistic. It seemed like I went from a dark area to a brighter area. My companion and the other missionaries we were living with were very upbeat, but I couldn't feel it on the inside. It was rather bizarre. I had hopes that over time my mood would elevate.

Unfortunately that did not occur. My mood actually got worse over time. I was getting very confused as I became more depressed. It just didn't make any sense. It was as if I had been in a long, cold rain storm and the sun quickly came and beautified my world. Yet I couldn't enjoy it. It was as if I wanted the storm to come back. This feeling reminded me of a scripture in the Book of Mormon (Mormon 9:4) which says: "Behold, I say unto you that ye would be more miserable to dwell with a holy and just God, under a consciousness of your filthiness before him, than ye would to dwell with the damned souls in hell." This didn't totally apply to me since I didn't feel filthy before the Lord but I still felt terrible.

I honestly thought that I would have felt better had I gone back to my previous area serving with the same companion. This strange, awful feeling should have made it easy to realize that I was truly depressed. I was surrounded by happy, carefree missionaries but I couldn't partake of the joy in the least bit. Instead, I was focused on being critical of the new area, my companion, and anything else that didn't seem to be just the way I thought it should be.

I wanted to be positive and tried to be, but my overall mood and demeanor seemed to put a huge damper on everyone around me, and I felt like I was making everyone else upset. From my journal, I felt cruddy one day and felt I was recovering the next. Once again, the mentioning of a "recovery" suggests that I needed intervention to get back to the way I was feeling several months before.

I felt I needed to pace myself. I had been working extremely hard ever since I entered the MTC. A friend of the family wrote me a letter, referencing Mosiah 4:27, which essentially says to not run faster than you have strength. He must have sensed that I had the strong potential to burn myself out. There's certainly nothing wrong with good hard work, but let's face it, you can overdo it. I love the quote from Brigham Young that mentions breaking up the day with eight hours of sleep, eight hours of work, and eight hours of play. I'm not sure how practical the play part is in our day, and it's certainly not practical as a full-time missionary, but the point that we need to take time to rest is a true principle. I've heard of people taking a work sabbatical for an entire year. That sounds like a dream to me right now.

As a 400-meter runner, I learned to go out fairly hard on the first 100 meters, maintain a good pace on the next 200 meters, and finally give it my all for the final 100 meters. Anybody who has tried to go out full speed for the first 200 meters of a 400-dash has learned the painful lesson that the last 200 meters will be much slower and very painful. No one can run 100-meter speed over the course of 400 meters. Is it possible that I dove into the mission field with 100-meter speed and burned myself out into depression? It certainly seems like a possible contributor.

The zone leader wanted to lose some weight before he went back home, and so he and some other missionaries and members went running most of the mornings at 5:30 am. Despite feeling they way I did, I went several times with them. One would think I would need to rest as much as possible in the mental state that I was in. Was my mood so low that it couldn't get any worse? That's a nice thought, but certainly not true. I despise the following quote but find it to be true: "No matter how bad it gets, it can always get worse." When it comes to moods, this translates to "no matter how bad you feel, you can always feel worse."

Despite feeling severely depressed, I was fortunate to maintain my physical abilities. This helped me maintain some needed self esteem.

I reflected on my father's mention of having the highest highs and lowest lows in the mission field. I hoped that I could go from a low to a high in the near future. As much as I wanted to get along with my companion and the other missionaries in our district, my negative mood continued to make things really difficult.

It was getting harder and harder to keep a fake smile on my face as I continued to attempt to share the gospel of peace and joy. Having the true gospel of Jesus Christ and the opportunity to share it should keep my mood as good as can be. Right? Unfortunately, at this time, things were just the opposite. I shouldn't kid myself into thinking that I was alone in having discouragement as a missionary. Unfortunately, discouragement was just part of what I was going through. I was sick!

One night my companion and the other missionary companionship called for a group discussion about how we can make things work better. I had already sensed that the other three were really having problems with me and I felt like none of them liked me. I was having problems liking myself at this time also. During this discussion I felt chewed up and spit out. The other missionaries were frustrated with me, as I acted as if there was no real problem. The other missionaries were trying to recall specific incidences where I was causing problems. It was kind of odd, since they really couldn't come up with specifics. My whole demeanor was the culprit.

We were all very frustrated. One of the missionaries said, "There's obviously a problem here," despite nobody really being able to explain exactly of what was going on. The truth of the matter was that I was clinically depressed, which can be a recipe for disaster in any setting. I felt like I was a repellant to everyone. I had bits and pieces of positivity in my journal, as I still hoped my mood would magically return to normal. I really wanted everything to work well, but it certainly wasn't. My frustrations grew, and I questioned in my journal, "When is this all going to end?"

One day my companion was sick, and we spent nearly an entire day at the apartment. I was feeling some physical sickness also. I pondered my past and how well my life had been going, until the last few months. I reflected on my life and looked at several old pictures of my family. I had several good memories as

I continued hoping for a better tomorrow. I occasionally would have a brief spurt of feeling okay, but was also frustrated as I felt we were not working hard enough.

I felt rather passive as a leader in the area since my companion had already been there. I didn't feel he was filling me in things as much as she should have. It was pretty routine for the senior companion to ride his bike ahead of the junior companion as the leader, but, because I didn't know the area, I had been riding behind my companion. Despite being the area leader and district leader, I didn't feel much like any kind of a leader.

One day I decided to ride in front of my companion. He really didn't like it and started biking really hard to pass me. We essentially raced back to the apartment. He wasn't able to catch me, and he was really upset. He tried to act like it didn't bother him much, but it really did. I mentioned in my journal that I "did major humbling on my companion and that I have plans to pick up the area and get it rolling." Shortly after the "bike race," I remember telling my companion that I was "there to humble him." He didn't seem to be too bothered by this as we had a decent day. I mentioned in my journal that I was becoming more optimistic and that I was getting along with my companion.

My mood and attitude took a small bump upward as I attended a couple of baptisms of people who I taught in a nearby area a few months before. However, the few good days with my companion were short lived. One day he just stopped talking to me. This led to another group companionship inventory with the four of us. I remember mentioning to the others that I really wanted the other three missionaries to have brotherly love toward me as I still felt like a bit of an outcast among them. Looking back, I can see how that would have been a rather difficult task for anyone at that time. After our discussion, I mentioned in my journal the need to repent and become the missionary I was before I got depressed. Repent? What did I need to repent of? I didn't feel I was breaking any commandments or mission rules. This depression had obviously caused a lot of guilt and confusion.

I was on assignment with the zone leader, who was one of the other missionaries that I lived with. He was upset and frustrated with how things were going. I could see how he might want to turn his back on me and act upset, but he really wanted to help me.

He was concerned about how I was feeling inside and told me about another missionary who had a "nervous breakdown." He specifically mentioned that this missionary was "very intense" and that he put a lot of pressure on himself to be the best missionary. I don't remember if this missionary went home early or not, but I remember saying to the zone leader something along the lines of, "Boy, I hope that doesn't happen to me." I remember telling myself this same thing several times. Little did I know that I was in the middle of a nervous breakdown, which I didn't realize was essentially the same thing as clinical depression.

I can't believe how long I had been in denial! I needed real help. I must have been like the black knight in the movie *Monte Python and the Holy Grail* when he had his arms and legs cut off and still thought he could defeat his opponent, King Arthur.

Similar to my previous area, I had another period of a few days where I was in that "hypomania" phase and actually felt surprisingly good. Just like the previous experience, it was short-lived and my deep depression symptoms returned quickly. I remember looking at others who were happy and feeling like, "It's not fair." I can imagine several others had looked at me with the same thought during the first 20 years of my life.

On Mother's Day (one of two days that missionaries are allowed to call home), I don't remember telling my parents much (if anything) about my depression. I do remember mentioning to my father that I was now the junior companion and he sounded really confused. That just didn't make sense to him. I had an idea why I was switched to junior companion (for my companion and me to get along better), but was embarrassed to tell my family. I remember saying something like, "Well, the mission president wants to give my companion an opportunity to be the senior companion."

Our zone was planning to have a fun day at the park, playing sand volleyball and other games. Normally, this would get me excited, but not this time. I just didn't want to do anything. I was clearly experiencing anhedonia, which is the inability to experience pleasure from activities usually found enjoyable. I would soon learn that this is a major sign of clinical depression.

When you think about it logically, anhedonia is totally messed up. I don't believe I had ever felt this frustrating feeling before the last few months. When I don't have any kind of a "go-to activity" to help improve my mood, what was I to do? The hopelessness can be compounded when a "fun activity" is attempted and it is not pleasurable at all. I don't remember much about that "fun" day except looking at several other missionaries enjoying themselves while I went through the motions, trying to act like I was having a good time.

Chapter 13: From Low to Lower

I mentioned in my journal that "my personality and character is shot" and that "I haven't been laughing much." Some time before this, as the district leader, I did a training session at a zone meeting while feeling depressed and didn't feel like it was helpful to anyone. The zone leader was very kind to say that I did a good job but I remained depressed throughout the day.

As the downward spiral of worsening mood continued I couldn't help but wonder if things were ever going to get better. It was getting more difficult to smile. I feared that by not smiling, people would ask me what was wrong or how I was feeling. I did not want anyone to know.

Let's get back to the "humbling statement" I made to my companion. I'm not entirely sure what I meant by that when I said it. All missionaries are most certainly going to be humbled many times throughout the course of a full-time mission, often by influence of a companion. Before the "humbling statement," I could argue that I had just physically humbled my companion during our bike race, which really should not mean much of anything. Is that all that I was referring to when I made the statement? It is probably not. Did I feel like I had a lot of things to teach him in the ways of missionary work? Of course I did. We all have much to teach one another.

What I meant at the time I said this to my companion does not really matter. What matters is how he interpreted it. He didn't act like he thought much about it initially, but it must have really affected him. Apparently he took it to mean something along the lines of me feeling that I was a superior missionary and that I had plans to be domineering. This was not the intended message. It obviously made him feel very small despite the fact that he is physically large and could put me into submission with a Tongan death grip at any given moment. I should be grateful this never happened.

I remember shortly after my "humbling comment" when my companion agreed that I was there to humble him. Had he changed his mind? I was just pleased that he started speaking to me again. It was looking like we were going to be getting along at that point.

This was very short lived. I didn't realize he had mentioned this concern to the others and then to the mission president as well. I was oblivious toward anything outside of the fact that he had stopped talking to me. The whole situation was becoming a little bizarre.

At the next zone conference, the mission president pulled me aside to discuss the concern of my companion. I remember him looking at me with a concerned look on his face as he said, "Your companion says that you told him you were here to humble him." I was a little confused about this because one of the last conversations I had with my companion was him coming to me and agreeing that I was there to humble him. So I looked back at my mission president with a bit of a confused look and said, "What? He came to me with that. That's the last thing he mentioned to me." We were obviously both confused. I remember mentioning that my companion, who was from Tonga, and who was speaking English as his second language, has got to be one of the most humble missionaries in the mission. The president agreed with me in this regard.

I don't remember much of the conversation beyond this, but I think this is when I must have been changed to a junior companion. I honestly don't remember being too upset about this. I may have even felt some relief. I don't remember things going any better or worse after this but in a very short period of time I was transferred on an emergent basis to another companion in a nearby area.

I was disappointed that things didn't go well with my companion and the others I lived with. I also felt like I was being punished to some degree. The only times I had heard about a missionary being emergency transferred was due to disobedience. I didn't feel like I had done anything disobedient. In regards to the "being punished" feeling, I would have to admit that I had felt like that for the last few months.

Chapter 14: Unexpected New Area

I didn't go far. I was in the same zone. I felt better in the sense that I was removed from a negative situation and had an opportunity to start again in a new area. I honestly don't believe being sent to a "better situation" would have made any difference. As much as I didn't want to admit it, my "joy circuit" was essentially "fried," as I was clinically depressed. My confidence of being able to "snap out of it" was diminishing. I felt I needed to stop worrying about accomplishments and leadership and get my act together. Although I was still depressed, at least I had pressure off from being the area leader and district leader.

One thing that I did enjoy at least a little about the new area was the weekly service that we did. Our district would go to the Orlando Humane Society to play with dogs on a weekly basis. I could take my mind off of how I felt for a short period of time.

My next monthly interview with the mission president went okay. We talked about possibly seeing a psychologist who was a local church member. This psychologist apparently was seeing other missionaries with similar concerns. I must have had at least a little burst of optimism as I mentioned in my journal that, "the second half of my mission will rock! I've got the skills, and the Lord is bound."

This hope was short-lived, as a journal entry shortly after this went as follows: "I'm going to go crazy or have a nervous breakdown soon. Good thing I'm used to stress and stuff. Doctor, doctor, check me out." I told the mission president and his wife to hook me up with the psychologist.

I was hopeful that the psychologist would know just what to do to get me feeling better. I thought he was a pretty cool guy, and in the end he physically humbled me. He whooped me in a push-up contest at the end of our visit. He thought my problem was essentially stemming from a "pride issue" and failed expectations. I guess his first step in helping me to be more humble was to beat me in a push-up contest.

I felt better when he mentioned that only the Savior didn't require therapy. He quoted Mosiah 4:10-11 about humility and how we as mortals are nothing compared to God. He committed me to writing my feelings in my journal each night and to pray more openly.

I told him that I'm very against taking any kind of medication. I don't know if telling him this influenced him, but in the end he said he didn't think I needed medication. That night I wrote that I definitely have a spiritual problem and have created a dam for myself.

Another interesting part of the visit was the color code personality test, which showed that I'm probably very difficult to read. I was a dead-even split amongst the three colors of red, blue, and yellow, and had just a little bit of white in me. Feel free to do some quick research on this.

My companion and I got along pretty well. This is partly because I was being much more passive. My companion didn't seem to want to talk to me much. I didn't feel like anybody really wanted to at the time. I still had the feeling like I was repellant to others. Don't get me wrong, it was normal as a missionary not to have much of a welcoming feeling from people as we went door to door. My feeling of rejection was now to a whole different level.

I was still feeling trapped or on a ball and chain. There were days when I felt really tired. One day I even took a 3-hour break. There was a period when I felt "really bad," which is significant since I was already feeling horrible. I felt like I was getting worse and needed to pray more. But no matter what I did I couldn't get feeling any better.

I was beginning to feel more scared as time went on. Was I ever going to feel well again? Being depressed, while in a position of spreading the joy of the gospel, made me feel like a hindrance to the work. In a strange journal entry, I mentioned I felt like my life was being flashed before me.

I felt that Satan and his angels were working hard to make me feel discouraged and depressed. I was becoming more fearful. I was straining my brain for how I could be doing things right but feeling so bad. I continually worried that I must not be worthy. I was feeling a loss of power in every way. I felt small and weak. I tried to laugh when sharing jokes with my companion but really couldn't. I had turned into a more passive missionary, yet I was still able to wear a fake smile and go through the motions.

As my mood got lower, my companion seemed to get a little more frustrated, which shouldn't have been a surprise. I think he was more confused about how I felt than anything. I didn't feel

43

so alone after he mentioned that he and some of his family members had been through counseling before.

Another disturbing journal entry: "I'm beginning to feel like I'm not one of the Lord's servants. And if so, dormant." On one particular Sunday I felt like I was "in hell to start the day but felt better after church." These small window periods of feeling okay must have been just enough to keep me going.

I found the book "The Power of Positive Thinking" somewhere in our apartment and read at least some of it. I don't remember it having much of an effect, but at least I had another pretty good day as I mentioned it in my journal. It may have been as good a day I'd had in the last three months.

My district leader opened up to me while we were going door to door and told me he had some of the same depressive symptoms at some point in the past. As this rough time went on, I was feeling bad about leaving a bad impression on others. I was a little anxious to go back to the psychologist. It's hard to determine how much help the first visit was. I may have been feeling just a little better at times than before, but mostly still depressed.

I retook the color code personality test at my second and final visit to the psychologist, and I had trouble answering the questions again. I even asked him for help on some of them. This time I ended up split between red and blue. I don't remember much more from our second visit with him but I think I came across as feeling a little better. He probably assumed that I was on the mend. We discussed pride again, as well as perfectionism, which I admitted I struggled with.

I had a few short periods when I felt like I was getting back to being happy again, and time was starting to pick up again. When depressed, time goes extremely slowly.

My mood dropped again shortly thereafter. My journal shows that I had recently been wondering who the heck I'm supposed to be and who the heck I am. I would occasionally feel some glimmers of hope. From journal: "I was receiving more answers to my problem, yet I was still mostly down and depressed. I need to lose myself in the work. This is one of many things I need to work on. My internal struggle has to end soon. It's difficult to help others be happy when I'm not."

It was a good thing that our district of four elders and two sisters got along well and had unity. We put a play together and performed it before a couple of large audiences in the Stake. The shows went really well. My emotions continued to be on a roller coaster of mostly lows and occasionally small bumps upward. Different feelings tended to flow through my body every day.

I hit another major downer one morning, and the elders of the district gave me a blessing of healing. I questioned if it should be a blessing of comfort or of healing and the district leader quickly stated that it definitely should be a blessing of healing.

On the next P-day, our zone got together, and it went okay. We played volleyball and had a barbeque. I still didn't feel well but was grateful to have a very caring district leader who could comfort me when I was most in need.

Chapter 15: Time to Start Over Again

At an interview with the mission president, he asked which companion I enjoyed serving with most. I told him it was either my trainer or one other companion. In the end, I told him my trainer. It became quite apparent why he asked. I was transferred to the Satellite Beach area, where my trainer was serving. Sure enough, I was joined with my trainer again. When I showed up, he was very surprised and said "I hatched you." I could tell he was somewhat concerned also. He knew I had been a leader in the mission, and now I was his junior companion.

This time serving with him would be different. When I was a new greenie, we pretty much went 100 mph. This time he had just one month to go, and I was battling depression; quite a different dynamic than before. Although our energy level was lower, we were much more experienced and smarter. On one of the early days with him in this new area, I was exhausted and fell asleep once or twice. The next morning I woke up depressed. I was finally getting to the point of fully admitting that I was battling major depression. My mother mentioned in a letter that she had a dream that I was ill. There was no question that I was sick.

The mission president and his wife determined that I needed to go to the doctor. My visit with the doctor was a little awkward. He was a family practitioner and was a member in the ward we were serving in. After telling him some of my symptoms he looked quite frustrated. I had the feeling that he was thinking to himself, "Great, one of the missionaries serving in the ward is depressed. I don't have any confidence referring any of my friends to hear the gospel from this missionary." I don't really know what he was thinking, but I was frustrated with him. He didn't seem too optimistic. I was frustrated that he didn't seem to have answers for me and that he wanted me to see someone else—a psychiatrist. He gave me samples of a medication called Effexor (generic name Venlafaxine) to start taking until I could see the psychiatrist. My companion called these my "happy pills."

I took one pill that very day, got really nauseated, and nearly vomited. I remember visiting a young member couple and they were really concerned how I looked. They came to the conclusion that I was probably just dehydrated. I didn't want to say, "I'm clinically depressed and just took a first pill and now I want to throw up." I went ahead and took another one the next day and I didn't feel good but wasn't quite as sick.

The next day I received a great package from my older brother. Normally, something like this would've given me a boost, but in my depressed state, it didn't cheer me up so much. Probably nothing would have.

The missionary work in the area was going pretty well. I was hopeful that I would feel well in the near future, but I continued to feel cruddy. One day I felt worse that I had a quite a while. There was really no reason for it other than the illness itself. I guess it is just the nature of the illness. I tried to comfort myself by reading my patriarchal blessing. I felt so upset, confused, and desperate. When is this going to end? Will it end? What do I have to do? My companion gave me a blessing of healing, and I can't ever remember crying so much.

My appointment with the psychiatrist wasn't to be for another three weeks unless somebody could pull some strings. The next day was zone conference. I felt like I was on my last thread most of the day. My companion was either speaking or doing some kind of training when he surprised me by having me read my mission call in front of all the missionaries in the zone. I was nearly in tears and was barely able to get through it.

The mission president sat down with me and he asked, "So do you feel like Job yet?" I remember pretty much telling him that I didn't know if I was doing any good out in the mission field and wondered if I should go home. I remember feeling that I could endure in my depressed state and grind though the mission, but this didn't seem like what the Lord would want me to do. The president and his wife, who happened to be a nurse, encouraged me to "hang in there." She mentioned one of their children having depression and that he benefitted from a book called "Feeling Good" by David D. Burns. It was kind of nice to read something besides the scriptures or the five books or so that we were allowed to read as missionaries.

Fortunately, I was able to see the psychiatrist much more quickly than initially scheduled. The visit was very positive. I remember him being very thorough in asking questions to help him get a more definitive diagnosis. Previous to this visit, I continually wondered if I was indeed clinically depressed. After the visit, there was no question. I may even have been considered a "textbook case" of clinical depression.

I don't remember what questions were asked, but every answer I gave suggested depression. The doctor said he would have started me on Prozac, but because I had already started the Effexor, I should just keep taking it. I was torn between the relief that I had a firm diagnosis with a treatment plan, and the fact that I was indeed clinically depressed. I told myself that I needed to think positive, forget about the past, and move forward.

If nothing else, depression had certainly humbled me. I became optimistic that I could fully recover and was confident that I would be a much better missionary when feeling well again. I made this comment in my journal: "Everyone's pulling for me, and of course the Lord is on my side. I know this is the end of my problem."

I was feeling a little better each of the next few days and then felt significantly better the morning of interviews with the mission president. He could tell I was feeling better and told me I should be ready to step it up with the missionary work.

A couple days later, as directed by the psychiatrist, the dose of my medication was increased as planned. I seemed to tolerate it just fine and was still optimistic that my mood would continue to improve.

Some days were better than others but overall I was getting progressively better. I was truly grateful that my mood was improving. My companion was happy about my improvement as well. He headed back home to Idaho on this good note.

CHAPTER 16: HOW IS DEPRESSION TREATED?

There are many options for the treatment of depression. In 10 years, there will probably be several more. It is vastly important to treat depression as early as possible and aggressively. Untreated depression can result in emotional, behavioral, and other health problems that affect every area of one's life.

For people who do not have any understanding of major depressive disorder (like me before the mission), the idea of treatment is probably to grab the depressed person by the shoulders, look him or her straight in the eye and say, "Come on, cheer up, you're not depressed. Stop being a pansy, square your shoulders, or pull yourself up by your bootstraps." Wouldn't it be nice if treatment were that easy? I am yet to see this approach work (unless your goal is to create a deeper level of depression).

A doctor isn't going to tell a diabetic patient to "will" their body's insulin production or one with high blood pressure to just "shake it off." Major depression, like diabetes or high blood pressure, needs to be treated appropriately.

Talk therapy is a first-line treatment—not buck-it-up talk. Cognitive behavioral therapy (CBT) has been shown to be most effective. I won't go into detail, but CBT is basically learning to recognize negative thinking patterns (cognitive distortions) and then learning to change the distorted thinking into healthy thought patterns. Several cognitive distortions are outlined in the book "Feeling Good, by David D. Burns." There are also many websites explaining CBT.

Medication is the other first-line treatment. In one of many studies, a large group of patients were treated with CBT (and no medicine) and another large group of patients were treated with medication only (no counseling of any kind). Both of these groups improved. So, what is the take-home message from this study? Taking medication and doing CBT needs to be investigated. As expected, studies have confirmed that doing both together works better than either treatment alone.

Many people still don't believe there's really such a thing as being clinically depressed. They think it's all in one's head (meaning no actual physiological changes). The fact that medication actually works far better than placebo suggests the opposite. Thousands of studies have proven the effectiveness of antidepressant medication.

I was quite skeptical about taking any kind of medication for depression. I wasn't one to trust medicine. Medications never seemed to really help me much with injuries, headaches, coughs, and the like. This reluctance to take medication more than likely delayed my healing process significantly. I would like to think that counseling (from the psychologist) did something for me, but looking back, it was the medicine (and pretty much the medicine alone) that worked for me. When I finally saw the family physician and then the psychiatrist, medication was the plan. The psychologist that I saw previously probably did a very good job, but my brain required medication that he couldn't prescribe.

A first-line medication for depression would be an SSRI (selective serotonin reuptake inhibitor). This class includes fluoxetine (Prozac), paroxetine (Paxil), sertraline (Zoloft), citalopram (Celexa), escitalopram (Lexapro), and fluvoxamine (Luvox). A newer medication called Viibryd acts as an SSRI and a serotonin agonist. The most recent SSRI (Trintellix) targets a number of serotonin receptors.

A very similar class would be the SNRI's (serotonin norepinephrine reuptake inhibitor) such as venlafaxine (Effexor), duloxetine (Cymbalta), desvenlafaxine (Pristiq), and livomilnacipran (Fetzema). There's an SNRI called atomoxetine (Strattera) that is indicated for attention deficit hyperactivity disorder and another SNRI called Savella that is indicated for Fibromyalgia. With the exception of these last two, any of these medications would also be considered first line.

Tricyclic antidepressants such as amitriptyline, nortriptyline, or imipramine work similar to SSRI's but tend to have more side effects and so have not been used as much in the last several years. MAOI's (monoamine oxidase inhibitors) are also rarely used due to their interactions with so many other medications, supplements, and foods, but are sometimes used in difficult to treat patients.

Bupropion (Wellbutrin) is indicated for Seasonal Affective Disorder (SAD—aka seasonal depression) as well as major depression, and is thought to help with the neurotransmitters norepinephrine and dopamine, and possibly a little with serotonin also.

Some antipsychotic medications such as aripiprazole (Abilify) or quetiapine (Seroquel) have been used as adjuncts to some of the previous medications listed. Wellbutrin is sometimes prescribed as an add-on also.

Another medical option is a low dose T3 (thyroid) medication which has been promising in some situations. A supplement called Deplin, which is folic acid based, has also been used as an adjunct to other antidepressants (typically SSRI or SNRI) as well.

Most of these medications require significant patience. Most do not begin to work for at least a few weeks. However, some of the newer ones may work faster and have lower side-effect profiles.

Several of my patients have felt like the medication they started taking worked almost immediately. It is my belief that most of these patients were optimistic that the medication would be working for them in a few weeks and so this excitement was already making them feel better. In other words, I think you can get an immediate placebo effect before physiologic brain changes occur from medication. To the contrary, some evidence suggests that physiological changes are seen in imaging even after the first dose of an antidepressant (although the clinical symptom relief does not occur this quickly).

Some recommendations from a doctor or therapist may include simplifying one's life by cutting back on obligations when possible, setting reasonable goals, and giving yourself permission to do less when you feel down.

Journal writing may also be part of treatment as it may help improve mood by allowing the patient to express pain, anger, fear, and other emotions. Self-help books or support groups have been helpful to some. Employee assistance programs and religious organizations may be good options for support as well.

Chapter 17: Senior Companion Again

It had been about a month since I started taking medication, and I was truly grateful that I was responding to it. I question whether I would have stayed in the mission field if I had not started feeling better. My mission president could also tell I was improving. I was called to be a senior companion again. It felt good to have a little more responsibility.

My companion was a young, "fireball" missionary who had been having a lot of success in the way of baptisms during his first several months. I had known him from a previous zone, and he always seemed to have a smile on his face. He seemed a little uncomfortable with me initially. Having gone through the last few months with deep depression and being "emergency transferred" I was quite certain he had heard negative things about me. I do not recall any discussion about this, and over time we got along just fine.

During our first few days together, I had some mild depression symptoms including some fatigue. This was most likely because I was adjusting to a new situation. This early funk seemed to fade, and my mood gradually improved as the days went on. We met an older couple eager to learn the gospel and had several other success stories as the weeks went on. My "highs" and "lows" were starting to feel more like they did before I got depressed. My mood didn't seem to be affected as much during the lows as it had in the recent past. In other words, it seemed like I was starting to feel more normal again.

I expressed gratitude in my journal after having a great day and feeling blessed. I expressed how my family had helped me so much and they truly are my strength. My companion and I continued to meet good people to teach and were having baptism success as well.

At one point I went on a temporary assignment with another missionary who was having similar depression symptoms. It was nice to have someone to empathize with. I loved teaching the gospel again, and time was going faster. Time goes so incredibly slow in a depressed state. The previous few months had felt like years to me. It felt good to have time moving more quickly again.

The next several days my mood continued to elevate. Missionary success continued to go strong. Had there not been much success in the way of missionary work, I really think my mood would have still elevated. I believe my brain was continuing to respond to the medication. Previous feelings of guilt and unworthiness had been swept away. After a few more great days, I mentioned in my journal that "I feel the rest of the mission will go light speed."

I was given the opportunity to serve with another new missionary right from the MTC. From the get-go, he seemed like a great missionary to serve with. For whatever reason, over the first few days my mood dropped down some. It made me wonder if I was on the right medication dose. I would later notice my depressive symptoms coming on whenever there were changes, such as a new companion or a new area.

Feeling somewhat depressed for a handful of days in a row was disturbing, but eventually the mood elevated back up. I got along well with my companion. We continued to have success. We enjoyed sharing previous athletic experiences and playing basketball on P-days. I served two months with this "greenie," and my mood generally improved as time went on. I had just a few scattered days of feeling tired or a little depressed. For the most part, I felt pretty well.

We had great discussions with some elect people, and I mentioned in my journal that "My testimony is as strong as ever." When I saw the psychiatrist again for a follow-up appointment, he mentioned that I looked much better. He said something about how my brow wasn't wrinkled like it was at the previous visit. The plan was to keep taking the same dose of medication.

CHAPTER 18: CONCERNS ABOUT MEDICATION

First of all, medication is not for everyone. As someone who had been anti-medication most of my life, I believed that avoiding medication was ideal. If someone can get feeling well again with counseling or other non-pharmacologic options, medication may not be needed. I'm more optimistic about non-pharmacologic options for those with milder depression. But even the more severely depressed patients may respond to non-pharmacologic treatment. It may be worth a try.

What if a medication doesn't work? This is not uncommon. Recommendations include increasing the dose or changing the medication, or even adding another medication.

What if a medication causes side effects? Just like any medication, the risks and benefits should be weighed carefully. Some medications, such as SSRIs, will sometimes cause initial side effects such as nausea, stomach ache, light-headedness, or headache. These symptoms usually go away shortly with time as the patient continues to take the medication. An intolerable side effect is a good reason to discontinue and try another option.

A medication may not work because the patient may not have clinical depression. Bipolar disorder, attention deficit hyperactivity disorder, schizophrenia, a personality disorder, etc, may not be affected by taking a typical antidepressant. Sometimes in bipolar patients, an antidepressant can even make a patient feel worse or even suicidal. When I was in physician assistant school doing a clinical rotation, a husband of a patient called the office where I was training to say how amazed and grateful he was that his wife, who was suffering from depression, was feeling so well, now that she was taking medication. The doctor that I was training with was happy to hear this and stated, "It's good to hear that I'm treating someone who really has depression and not some personality disorder." One lesson: Some patients seek certain medications that are not necessarily appropriate for them.

Take, for instance, someone who simply doesn't like his or her life, possibly due to poor decision making or bad luck. If the patient doesn't have physiologic brain changes, then a medication wouldn't do any better than a placebo, and may cause some unwanted side effects. If someone feels normal (not clinically depressed), then taking an antidepressant will not enhance his or her mood. Medicine is for sick people!

When I spoke with someone selling life insurance, he asked me if I took any medications. When I said that I was taking antidepressant medication he replied, "Oh, okay, so you take something to take off the edge?" I pretty much agreed to avoid having to explain that I would be severely depressed if I was not taking the medication. Once again, medicine is for sick people. I do not recommend taking a medication just to "take off the edge."

What about the common fear of addiction? None of the medications that I have mentioned are potentially addictive. Can you be dependant on one or more of these medications? Sure. If I had outrageously high blood pressure, I should have no problem depending on a medication to keep me from having a stroke or a heart attack. If I had low thyroid, I would have no problem being dependant on a thyroid supplement so I wouldn't be gaining weight or feeling cold and dead tired. Why should it be different with depression and taking an antidepressant? Don't get me wrong, there most certainly are prescription medications that are addictive. I believe these should be used sparingly and only when necessary.

Some patients will say they don't want to take a medication because it's just a band-aid or a crutch that is merely covering up a problem and masking their feelings. I can understand these thoughts. Avoiding medication is typical human nature. On the flip side, a medication can be extremely helpful. The people who feel medication is "just a band-aid" are usually the same people who think depression is a "weakness" and those that suffer from it need to toughen up. The stigma of depression is still prevalent, but not as much as in previous years. I don't fault anyone for their misconceptions; I was there once too.

Take this obvious analogy. If I had a patient dying from terminal cancer and in extreme pain, I don't think it would make sense to withhold pain "band-aid" medication from him or her because "they're supposed to be feeling that way." That's just silly.

Is a band-aid a bad thing? Is a crutch a bad thing? Of course not. If you can't put pressure on one of your feet, a crutch can be very useful. Is that covering up a problem? I would say it is being used to manage a problem, similar to a medication being used to manage an illness. I don't think of patients covering up their diabetes problem with insulin because they require it to live.

Is depression something "you're supposed to be feeling?" As I mentioned earlier, depression can be a healthy emotional response just like physical pain, but a persistent clinical depression is an illness that needs to be treated and will usually get worse if not treated in a timely manner.

If I burn my hand on a hot stove, I would be grateful for the brief pain telling me to remove my hand so it doesn't become badly burned. If I injure my knee, causing major damage to some of the structures, and I can't walk on it without severe pain, I am not grateful for this pain, and I do not plan on repeatedly walking on it "because I should be feeling the pain." I would have no problem resting it, icing it, elevating it, and wearing a knee brace if that would help. If you want to call this treatment plan for my knee "covering up a problem," then I don't know if I'm getting through to you.

It's not uncommon for a patient to tell me when he or she used to take an antidepressant, "it took my emotions away" or similarly, "I felt like a zombie because it totally leveled my emotions." In my opinion, if that is the case, I would say that these patients were probably on the wrong medication or might not have needed medication.

What I'm about to say may sound kind of weird, but someone feeling severely depressed would gladly take a loss of emotions as a big upgrade over not wanting to live. Although I never had a medication affect me that way, I would've welcomed the "zombie feeling" over severe depression.

Lastly, most antidepressants have a black box warning due to the possible side effect of suicidal ideation, more likely in adolescents and young adults. There is much debate about whether antidepressants really cause people to commit suicide. One possibility is that a patient can be so low and depressed that taking an antidepressant can give the patient just enough energy to carry out the suicidal thoughts. This is known as a paradoxical reaction. I have been fortunate to not come across this situation since I've been in practice. I do believe this is a possibility (because you never say never in medicine), but, in general, antidepressants rarely (if ever?), cause suicide.

It's easy to make a correlation between antidepressants and suicide since most people taking antidepressants are suffering from depression and practically the only people committing suicide are clinically depressed. But the correlation does not prove cause and effect, any more than having an auto crash correlate to having a driver's license. If I researched 100 patients who committed suicide and found that the majority of them had taken or were currently taking one or more antidepressants, should I be surprised? Of course not. That doesn't mean the antidepressants caused suicide. Being severely depressed caused suicide! Some of them may have been further depressed because they tried one or more antidepressants and didn't get feeling better, and so they became further frustrated and depressed. I will further discuss the problem of suicide in chapter 23.

Chapter 19: Transferred

It was mid-October and I was transferred back to Bradenton; this time to the area adjacent to my second area in the mission field. I knew my companion from earlier in the mission, and we worked together well. I may have felt just a little depressed briefly due to adjustment, but we were having success and my optimism continued. I was the area leader and district leader again, but this time I wasn't feeling a lot of stress.

Things seemed to be going smoothly, and I was grateful. While in this area, some other missionaries were talking about depression. I was able to share quite a bit of useful information with them. My overall attitude toward other people had changed entirely. I felt much more able to help anyone who seemed to be struggling emotionally to any degree. Before, I was quite limited in feeling empathetic toward those with depression.

During the last several months of the mission, I taught a number of the people who seemed to have been placed in my path because of my experience. I was prepared to help them because of the "new" me.

Today, I often tell my patients that in regards to health, no news is usually good news. Many great things occurred while I served in this area of Bradenton. Fortunately, very little of it has much to do with my illness of depression. The further I get from those awful months, the easier it is to put out of my mind and move forward.

CHAPTER 20: ALTERNATIVE TREATMENTS

Some alternative treatments include supplements such as St. John's Wort or SAMe. Some research shows St. John's Wort being helpful, but other research shows that it was no better than a placebo. It's thought to have a mild action similar to an SSRI. SAMe is a supplement that has also been used for years. It has also been shown to have a mechanism of action similar to that of an SSRI or tricyclic antidepressant. Omega 3 fatty acids (fish oils) have shown to help with depression in some research.

There are many other supplements claiming to help depression, but not much concrete research to back them up. Because of the lack of research, you can waste a lot of time and money trying to find a supplement to help depression. I'm not saying it's not possible, but I would go with the proven treatments.

Mind-body techniques such as yoga, tai chi, meditation, guided imagery, affirmations, breathing exercises, music, and art therapy have all shown positive effects in some people. Acupuncture or massage may help as well. I recommend these be used as adjuncts to psychotherapy or medication or both.

Physical exercise is something everyone should be doing, whether depressed or not. Unfortunately, people suffering from depression often do not feel they can exercise. I recommend starting with something very simple and working up from there. Physical activity has been shown to help depression in most cases. Exercise would probably be more beneficial to someone who is more sedentary when depression sets it. In other words, if my patient is actively exercising while becoming depressed, I wouldn't bank on more exercise as a cure for that individual.

I was very active at the time I came down with depression and this may be why exercise never seemed to help my mood. In fact, it has made it worse at times. I certainly recommend exercise to everyone, especially those with depression or anxiety, because it has shown to help in most cases. I may be an outlier in this regard.

Diet is nearly always discussed with exercise. Certain foods may have an effect of increasing serotonin, which suggests some benefits in depression. A healthy diet in general is certainly recommended. Regarding serotonin, there has to be more factors involved in depression than just serotonin. If not, serotonin injections or infusions would probably be options (They are not).

59

Remember, SSRI medications often take four to six weeks to start working.

Other antidepressants, sometimes called atypical antidepressants, such as nefazodone (Serzone) and trazodone (Desyrel) work differently than SSRIs and can be used to treat the same symptoms. I don't have a good explanation for this except that it has to be much more complicated than serotonin alone.

Biofeedback and neurofeedback have each been shown to help depression as well as other mental illnesses. These may be a little pricey, but certainly worth doing if effective.

Electroconvulsive therapy (ECT) has been very effective but is not used much due to relapse if not done regularly. There are also possible side effects such as memory loss. Transcranial magnetic stimulation (TMS) is somewhat similar to ECT but without the extreme measure of inducing a brief seizure.

A more extreme measure involving a surgery called vagal nerve stimulation is another option if other treatments are not effective.

An injection of Ketamine has been shown to be rapidly effective for depression, but I've only read about it. I can see it being a more viable option in the future.

Apparently there may be an option of botox also. I'm not really sure how this works either. With so many treatment options, it surprises to me how the rates of clinical depression continue to rise. I am hopeful this trend will turn around in the future.

Chapter 21: Final Area

I was transferred to Fort Myers for my last area. My companion was initially quiet and seemed a little distant. Similar to previous transfers I had some short periods of mild depression during the first few days.

We had a great P-day bowling with several other missionaries on the first week. I was a little disturbed, though, because I could tell some of the other missionaries in the district had heard some rumors about me. Instead of inquiring what they may have heard, I just went about my merry way and treated everyone with kindness and respect. Things smoothed over as time went by.

My companion and I got along well. He was quite a prankster. Just like the two previous areas, the missionary success was moving along well. I had a few short dips in mood, most likely due to mild frustrations within the district, but overall was doing well.

With just three months to go, I was given another greenie companion from the MTC. He was fairly quiet and seemed to have a difficult time adjusting to being a missionary.

I continued to take my medication as directed. Despite feeling much better on the medication, I really did not like feeling dependant on it. I certainly hoped that I wouldn't need to take it much longer. I had only two office visits with the psychiatrist, but he was nice enough to let me call him on occasion.

I felt very strongly about trying to stop the medication. This shouldn't be a surprise since it took months of denial before I considered taking a medication. At one of my visits, the psychiatrist told me that I should take my medication for at least nine to 12 months. I had been taking it for close to nine months, and since I had been feeling fairly well, I asked him if I could stop the medication. He explained that this type of medication is not to be stopped abruptly and that one is supposed to slowly taper off the medication. I remember hearing some concern in his voice in discussing tapering off the medication, but he still gave me the go ahead.

My dose for the last several months was a 75 mg tablet in the morning and ½ tablet (37.5 mg) in the afternoon or evening. During the tapering process I was quite excited about feeling well as I went to ½ tab twice a day for a week or so, and then ½ tab in the morning and ¼ tab in the pm for another week or so. The next step was to take just ¼ tab twice a day, then ¼ tab once a day for a while and then stop.

Part of me thought my mood would drop just a little bit each time I decreased the dose, but this did not happen at all. I felt fine during the entire tapering process, even when I was taking just ¼ tab each day. Unfortunately, shortly after stopping all medication, my depression symptoms started to come back.

As anyone would expect, I was very disappointed that I was starting to feel depressed again. It's amazing how quickly I had forgotten how bad I felt for those awful months. I think it is human nature to forget negative things from the past. I can't think of anything more negative than depression.

Fortunately, after going back to my "regular dose" of 75 mg in am and 37.5 mg in pm, my mood returned to near normal after about a week.

This was certainly a relief, yet I still didn't like being dependant on medication. As expected, time went by much more quickly. My mood was okay for the last few months.

I was truly grateful that I was able to finish the two-year mission. As badly as I felt during the mid part of the mission, it was nothing short of a miracle that I could effectively serve the last several months.

My parents were thrilled to see me looking happy and healthy on my return home. As planned, I did some serious resting, mostly on my parents' couch, for at least two weeks in recovery from the exhausting life of a missionary. Similar to other transfers I did feel a little depressed for a while adjusting to post mission life. As time went on, and I continued to take my medication, my mood stabilized again. It was time to get back into the college scene.

CHAPTER 22: HOW DO YOU PREVENT DEPRESSION?

To prevent depression, you need to know and understand the possible causes. Also, just like other medical concerns, you would want to get help as early as possible. If you're in an acute, stressful situation, getting help may simply mean taking a vacation or getting away from whatever is causing the symptoms. Getting plenty of sleep and avoiding alcohol and drugs are also shown to prevent depression.

Is depression contagious? That may sound silly, but in a sense it certainly can be, although not like an infectious disease. When one member of an intimate relationship comes down with depression, it is quite common for the other to become depressed also. In other words, if you're hanging out with depressed people, you're more likely to become depressed. I wouldn't completely avoid being around people who are depressed, but I recommend limiting the amount of time spent with them. Associating more with people who are cheerful, happy, and upbeat can have a positive effect on mood.

I mentioned earlier the possibility of depression coming from selfishness or pride. I guess that would suggest being humble could prevent depression. That doesn't mean you shouldn't "joy in your success." I don't think so. I believe you should feel satisfaction from your good works and even celebrate at times.

Depression has a strong genetic link, but you can't change your parents. Do the best with what you have. Another challenge might be one's personality. I mentioned "The Color Code" earlier. Those who are strong in the blue color are more likely to get depressed. I mentioned earlier that I was a split between, red, blue, and yellow, and then split between red and blue. It's more clear now that I'm mostly a blue (and not just because I went to BYU).

One good prevention measure is to avoid becoming isolated. Try participating in social activities and getting together with family and friends regularly. Do your best to take care of yourself. Eat a healthy diet, be physically active, and get plenty of sleep. Learn ways to relax and manage stress.

I have another theory about depression susceptibility, which is, "The bigger they are, the harder they fall." I'm not talking about size in this case, I'm talking about fame. I've never been to a third world country, but have been told that the children there are often happy despite having so little. They don't know any better. Childhood actors, on the other hand, usually are dealing with more than they can handle. Of course they look (and usually are) very happy when they're "on top of the world." Then what happens? As far as I'm concerned, they have only one direction to go after they get to the top.

How often do you hear a happy story about a childhood actor after his or her fame runs out? Most probably have no plan after their time in the spotlight. They probably think they'll always be on top. It is my opinion that those who develop addictions to drugs or alcohol have often turned to these vices as self-treatment for depression. It's unfortunate how often we hear about childhood actors ending up in rehab, with some of them taking their own lives.

This pattern is certainly not limited to childhood actors. Adult actors, singers, athletes, high profile figures, and even lottery winners are vulnerable. I am generally a believer in the principle of having "moderation in all things."

CHAPTER 23: SUICIDE

I really tried to avoid writing a chapter on suicide. Unfortunately, if depression is not treated appropriately, some lives end in suicide. I do not like to think about this. It is a very scary subject to me. Before I became depressed, suicide made absolutely no sense to me at all. Who in the world would want to kill himself or herself? Why do females attempt suicide three times as often as males? Why are males three times more likely to successfully carry out a suicide? Why are adolescents and young adults becoming more likely to commit suicide? On the flip side, why is the group with the highest risk of suicide males over the age of 85?

Unfortunately, after experiencing significant depression, the thought of suicide made a lot more sense to me. It is very possible to feel bad enough for long enough to want to die. If not so, suicide would not be a problem.

There is a medical condition called trigeminal neuralgia that causes extreme facial pain. It used to be called "suicide disease" because the uncontrollable pain would cause a very high percentage of patients to take their own lives. The treatments for this are better today, and there is far less suicide from it. It makes good sense that a medical condition causing uncontrollable physical pain could lead to people taking their own lives.

I personally do not suffer from any chronic pain nor do I recall being in severe pain for any significant period of time. In other words, I cannot empathize very well with chronic pain sufferers, as I can only <u>imagine</u> what they are going through.

Before I believed and knew that clinical depression was a real thing, I had absolutely no idea what a depression sufferer felt inside. With depression going from mild to moderate to severe, it makes sense that it could get bad enough and out of control, similar to a physical pain, to cause one to take his or her life.

There are some suicidal thoughts that I do not consider to be rare. Having a few really bad days might trigger a thought such as..."What if I turn this wheel and my car just went off the edge of this cliff or bridge?" Fortunately these fleeting thoughts rarely lead to serious plans, but they could.

I've had a handful of patients (who I would not consider to be suicidal) who would mention to me that they feel jealous while reading the obituaries in the newspaper. I would put this in a similar category with the fleeting thoughts of turning the wheel.

Don't get me wrong, these types of thoughts are very serious. Major help is essential to avoid the kinds of thoughts that lead to plans for suicide attempts. If you or a loved one is having serious suicidal thoughts, go directly to the emergency room for immediate crisis intervention.

From a religious standpoint, suicide, like murder, is considered a very serious sin. I have thought quite a bit about this. I've had some thoughts about accountability. I've always been taught that young children and those with severe mental deficits need no baptism because they are not accountable like mature adults. I've wondered if it were possible that a knowledgeable adult could go from being fully accountable to no longer accountable because of severe depression. It is my belief that this is possible and that several people who have taken their own lives were "not in their right mind."

I found comfort in reading M. Russell Ballard's talk in the October General Conference in 1987 titled "Suicide: Some Things We Know, and Some We Do Not." In this talk he mentions how previous church leaders have hinted that "persons subject to great stresses may lose control of themselves and become mentally clouded to the point that they are no longer accountable for their acts. Such are not to be condemned for taking their own lives." I've always been bothered by those who judge suicide victims to be selfish for having committed such a heinous sin. As far as I'm concerned, every situation is different. "Judgment is the Lord's; He knows the thoughts, intents, and abilities of men; and He in His infinite wisdom will make all things right in due course."

The bottom line is that everything should be done to help anyone looking to take his or her own life. Those who do take their own life should not be judged by man.

CHAPTER 24: REMISSION

No. I'm not referring to immediately going on another mission. I'm referring to the happy side of any daunting medical diagnosis. Remission: A diminution of the seriousness or intensity of disease or pain; a temporary recovery.

I usually hear the term remission in reference to being free from cancer. Being in remission from cancer is most certainly a happy thing since the initial diagnosis of cancer most likely creates future uncertainty. Some people will say that they hope for the best but prepare for the worst. Remission would be the best scenario and chronic depression or death would be the worst.

For depression, remission is most certainly the goal. I am referring to complete remission, that is. Partial remission is definitely better than no remission, but the goal is complete remission.

To put it in simple terms, remission from depression is essentially equivalent to feeling normal. Depression—bad. Normal—good. Remission is the happiest and best possible outcome of chronic major depressive disorder. The other side of the spectrum would be severe depression leading to suicide. Like I said before, getting toward this end of the spectrum is terrifying, as the feelings of control diminish. This is why I feel it is so important to receive any and every treatment option to maximize the possibility of remission.

Once in remission, the goal is to stay there…forever. This doesn't mean bad things aren't going to happen or there won't be bad days or weeks. That's called life. It does mean overcoming and continuing to be free from those awful symptoms of anhedonia, deep depression, hopelessness, and not wanting to live.

Chapter 25: Going Forth With Stability

My transfer to home was somewhat similar to the last few transfers in mission field where my mood would drop a little during a short adjustment period. One big difference is that I didn't have anything I had to do right away. I pretty much lied on the couch every day for about two weeks. Despite my mood dropping down a little, I certainly felt joy deep down inside, having completed a successful two-year mission. It was certainly the hardest thing I had ever done.

Just as being a missionary was new territory, being a returned missionary was new territory. After my couch period and watching a few ball games that my dad recorded while I was gone, I got a summer job washing and detailing cars. After giving a homecoming address to the ward I grew up in and a few other talks, I began to attend the singles branch. It felt a little weird, and it was an adjustment talking to girls without the main intent of encouraging them to read The Book of Mormon.

My mood was still a bit of a struggle at times. On a particular night, it was difficult to enjoy going to a Seattle Mariners baseball game. The only other time I can remember feeling terrible at a Mariners game was in my youth after overdosing on Skittles and Starburst. I found quotes in my journal of saying, "Depression is Lame," and "When's life gonna get easy?" Listening to Chariots of Fire music seemed to help a little. After a few dates, catching up with some old friends, watching some movies, working, and a family vacation, it was time to head back to BYU in the fall of 1997.

A part of me questions whether my adjustment period was much different than any returned missionary who never struggled with depression. I'd like to fully believe the latter, but I couldn't deny that my emotional well being was still compromised at least somewhat.

On the bright side, any depressive symptoms that I experienced after being home from the mission paled in comparison to the deep darkness experienced in the middle of the mission. Transitioning back into college, playing sports, dating, and church activity seemed to be as smooth as I could have hoped for considering how badly I felt just about a year before. Suffice it to say, that I felt like I succeeded in achieving remission from depression. If not complete remission, at least really close. It felt great to feel "normal" again.

CONCLUSION

After what I would call an ideal childhood and a very great and productive first several months of a full-time church mission, an unexpected depression took me down. I felt like I was hanging from a thread. I didn't feel something like this was possible. I certainly didn't see it coming. My hope diminished the longer the depression continued. I questioned many times whether I could ever feel normal again. Fortunately, with help from medication, I was able to regain a semblance of a normal, productive life. I do not like to think about what might have happened had I not benefitted from treatment.

The way I responded to medication after being severely depressed as a missionary was nothing short of a miracle. I couldn't believe how low my mood could go and yet, in a relatively short period of time, it came back up pretty close to normal. I am indeed grateful to have regained the light necessary to complete a two-year mission.

I am filled with gratitude as I had heard stories of, and seen many others who have been unable to recover from major depression. Some of these people are no longer alive in mortality. There have been many who have suffered from depression, there are many who suffer now, and there will continue to be those who suffer in the future.

There is nothing good about depression. It is miserable. It's real, it's possible, and it could happen to anyone. But fortunately it is treatable. Because of this, do not lose faith in yourself or others.

For those of you who have personally battled and overcome depressive symptoms, kudos for you! For those who have helped others overcome these battles, kudos for you too! Whether the help came from psychotherapy, supplements, yoga, lifestyle changes, or medication, it doesn't matter. Good for you. Feeling well is feeling well.

For those who are still battling, hang in there. Know that depression is treatable. Get all the help you can. If on medication, do not be embarrassed. Others may judge you, but they do not understand. Let that be their problem and not yours. When in remission it is my belief that helping others who have suffered from depression will help to keep you in remission.

Made in the USA
Coppell, TX
17 December 2020

45786927R00042